The Song of Harvest

Bob Chilcott

for SATB and organ

vocal score

MUSIC DEPARTMENT

OXFORD
UNIVERSITY PRESS

OXFORD
UNIVERSITY PRESS

Great Clarendon Street, Oxford OX2 6DP,
United Kingdom

Oxford University Press is a department of the University of Oxford.
It furthers the University's objective of excellence in research, scholarship,
and education by publishing worldwide. Oxford is a registered trade mark of
Oxford University Press in the UK and in certain other countries

© Oxford University Press 2021

Bob Chilcott has asserted his right under the Copyright, Designs
and Patents Act, 1988, to be identified as the Composer of this Work

First published 2021

Impression: 1

ISBN 978-0-19-355775-8

Music and text origination by Katie Johnston

Printed in Great Britain on acid-free paper by
Halstan & Co. Ltd, Amersham, Bucks.

Contents

Composer's note

Harvest season is a special time of the year. Living as I do in quite a rural part of England, each year we become ever more aware of the passing of the seasons, of the weather patterns, and also of the changing colours and textures of the land around us. After the challenges that we have all faced in 2020 and 2021, I wanted to write a simple expression to reflect on some thoughts of how the concept of harvest might relate to us all as we move forward, through sustainability, community, giving, hope, care, and, perhaps most importantly, thankfulness.

I was not specifically looking to write a stand-alone work, but rather a piece that could be equally performed as one or simply delved into and movements or hymns sung separately. It was written for the Royal School of Church Music Celebration Day, held at Durham Cathedral on 9 October 2021, as part of a day to celebrate what it means to sing together. I am grateful to Hugh Morris, Director of the RSCM, to Daniel Cook, Master of the Choristers and Organist of Durham Cathedral, and to my dear friend who supported the creation of this work.

Duration: *c.*26 minutes

This note may be reproduced as required for programme notes.

Texts

These texts and melodies may be reproduced as required for programme notes and to allow audience/congregation participation in the hymns during a performance of *The Song of Harvest*.

1. Hymn: Come, ye thankful people, come

Music: Bob Chilcott; Words: Henry Alford (1810–71)

MORRIS

1. Come, ye thankful people, come,
   Raise the song of harvest-home!
   All be safely gathered in,
   Ere the winter storms begin;
   God, our Maker, doth provide
   For our wants to be supplied;
   Come to God's own temple, come;
   Raise the song of harvest-home!

2. We ourselves are God's own field,
   Fruit unto his praise to yield;
   Wheat and tares together sown,
   Unto joy or sorrow grown;
   First the blade and then the ear,
   Then the full corn shall appear;
   Grant, O harvest Lord, that we
   Wholesome grain and pure may be.

3. For the Lord our God shall come,
   And shall take his harvest home;
   From his field shall purge away
   All that doth offend, that day;
   Give his angels charge at last
   In the fire the tares to cast,
   But the fruitful ears to store
   In his garner evermore.

4. Then, thou Church triumphant, come,
   Raise the song of harvest-home;
   All be safely gathered in,
   Free from sorrow, free from sin,
   There for ever purified
   In God's garner to abide;
   Come, ten thousand angels, come,
   Raise the glorious harvest-home!

2. This is the day

Psalm 118: 24, 28–9

This is the day which the Lord hath made: we will rejoice and be glad in it.
Thou art my God, and I will thank thee: thou art my God, and I will praise thee.
O give thanks unto the Lord, for he is gracious: and his mercy endureth for ever.

3. Hymn: For the beauty of the earth

Music: Bob Chilcott; Words: F. S. Pierpoint (1835–1917)

EXON

1. For the beauty of the earth,
   For the beauty of the skies,
   For the love which from our birth
   Over and around us lies:
   Christ our God, to thee we raise
   This our sacrifice of praise. [repeat]

2. For the beauty of each hour
   Of the day and of the night,
   Hill and vale, and tree and flow'r,
   Sun and moon and stars of light:
   Christ our God, to thee we raise
   This our sacrifice of praise. [repeat]

3. For the joy of human love,
   Brother, sister, parent, child,
   Friends on earth, and friends above,
   For all gentle thoughts and mild:
   Christ our God, to thee we raise
   This our sacrifice of praise. [repeat]

4. For each perfect gift of thine
   To our race so freely giv'n,
   Graces human and divine,
   Flow'rs of earth and buds of heav'n:
   Christ our God, to thee we raise
   This our sacrifice of praise. [repeat]

4. Gratitude

Henry van Dyke (1852–1933)

Whatever gifts and mercies in my lot may fall,
I would not measure
As worth a certain price in praise, or great or small;
But take and use them all with simple pleasure.

For when we gladly eat our daily bread, we bless
The Hand that feeds us;
And when we tread the road of Life in cheerfulness,
Our very heart-beats praise the Love that leads us.

5. Hymn: Pray that Jerusalem may have peace

Music: Bob Chilcott; Words: Scottish Psalter (1650)

PATE

(organ)

1. Pray that Jerusalem may have
   Peace and felicity:
   Let them that love thee and thy peace
   Have still prosperity.

2. Therefore I wish that peace may still
   Within thy walls remain,
   And ever may thy palaces
   Prosperity retain.

3. Now, for my friends' and brethren's sake,
   Peace be in thee, I'll say;
   And for the house of God our Lord
   I'll seek thy good alway.

6. King of Glory, King of Peace

George Herbert (1593–1633), from The Temple *(1633)*

King of Glory, King of Peace,
I will love thee:
And that love may never cease,
I will move thee.
Thou hast granted my request,
Thou hast heard me:
Thou didst note my working breast,
Thou hast spared me.

Wherefore with my utmost art
I will sing thee,
And the cream of all my heart
I will bring thee.
Though my sins against me cried,
Thou didst clear me;
And alone, when they replied,
Thou didst hear me.

Sev'n whole days, not one in sev'n,
I will praise thee.
In my heart, though not in heav'n,
I can raise thee.

7. Hymn: Through all the changing scenes of life

Music: Bob Chilcott; Words: Nahum Tate (1652–1715) and Nicholas Brady (1659–1726), New Version of the Psalms of David (1696)

MANNERS

1. Through all the changing scenes of life,
   In trouble and in joy,
   The praises of my God shall still
   My heart and tongue employ.

2. O magnify the Lord with me,
   With me exalt his name;
   When in distress to him I called,
   He to my rescue came.

3. The hosts of God encamped around
   The dwellings of the just;
   Deliv'rance he affords to all
   Who on his succour trust.

4. O make but trial of his love,
   Experience will decide
   How blest they are, and only they,
   Who in his truth confide.

5. Fear him, ye saints, and you will then
   Have nothing else to fear;
   Make you his service your delight,
   Your wants shall be his care.

6. To Father, Son, and Holy Ghost,
   The God whom we adore,
   Be glory, as it was, is now,
   And shall be evermore. Amen.

8. Consider

Christina Rossetti (1830–94)

Consider
The lilies of the field whose bloom is brief:
We are as they;
Like them we fade away,
As doth a leaf.

Consider
The sparrows of the air of small account:
Our God doth view
Whether they fall or mount,
He guards us too.

Consider
The lilies that do neither spin nor toil,
Yet are most fair:
What profits all this care
And all this coil?

Consider
The birds that have no barn nor harvest-weeks;
God gives them food:
Much more our Father seeks
To do us good.

9. Hymn: Now thank we all our God

Music: Bob Chilcott; Words: Martin Rinkart (1586–1649), trans. Catherine Winkworth (1827–78)

PICKER

1. Now thank we all our God,
   With heart and hands and voices,
   Who wondrous things hath done,
   In whom this world rejoices;
   Who from our mother's arms
   Hath blessed us on our way
   With countless gifts of love,
   And still is ours today.

2. O may this bounteous God
   Through all our life be near us,
   With ever joyful hearts
   And blessed peace to cheer us;
   And keep us in his grace,
   And guide us when perplexed,
   And free us from all ills
   In this world and the next.

3. All praise and thanks to God
   The Father now be given,
   The Son, and him who reigns
   With them in highest heaven,
   The One eternal God,
   Whom earth and heav'n adore;
   For thus it was, is now,
   And shall be evermore. Amen.

Commissioned for the Royal School of Church Music
*with the generous support of an anonymous donor and dedicated to all those
who work so hard to sustain church music now and into the future*

The Song of Harvest

1. Hymn: Come, ye thankful people, come

Henry Alford (1810–71)

BOB CHILCOTT

'MORRIS'

win - ter storms be - gin; God,__ our Mak - er, doth__ pro - vide

For__ our wants__ to be__ sup - plied; Come__ to God's own

tem - ple, come; Raise__ the song__ of har - vest - home!

S. A.

2. We__ our - selves__ are God's__ own field,__
3. For__ the Lord__ our God__ shall come,__

T. B.

2. This is the day

Psalm 118: 24, 28–9

BOB CHILCOTT

This is the day which the

Lord_____ hath made: we will re - joice and be glad in it.

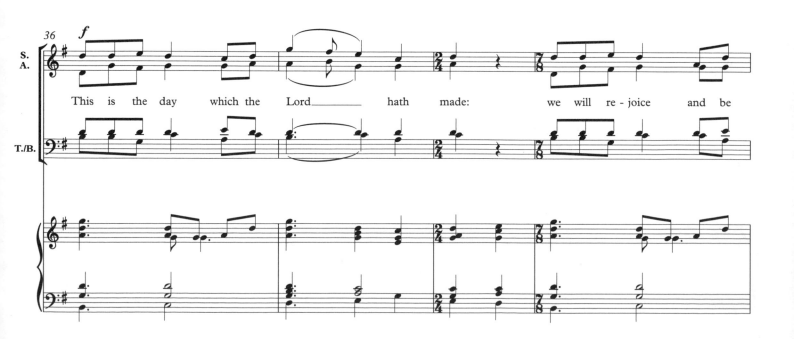

This is the day which the Lord_____ hath made: we will re - joice and be

glad in it, glad in it, glad_____ in it.

mp poco espress.

O give thanks un-to the Lord, for he is gra-cious,

mp poco espress.

O_____ give thanks, for he is gra - cious: and his

glad in it. This is the day which the Lord_____ hath

made: we will re - joice and be glad in it,

glad in it, glad_____ in it._____

3. Hymn: For the beauty of the earth

F. S. Pierpoint (1835–1917)

BOB CHILCOTT

'EXON'

flow'r, Sun and moon and stars of light: *Christ our God, to thee we raise This our*

moon and stars of light:

sa - cri - fice of praise, *Christ our God, to thee we raise This our*

sa - cri - fice of praise.

3. For the

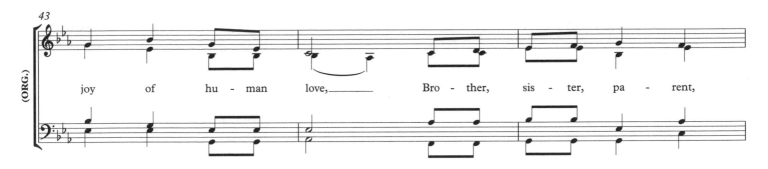

joy of hu - man love,_____ Bro - ther, sis - ter, pa - rent,

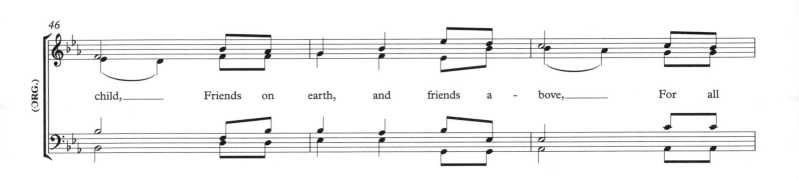

child,_____ Friends on earth, and friends a - bove,_____ For all

gen - tle thoughts and_____ mild:_____ *Christ our God,_____ to thee we raise_____ This our*

53 sa - cri - fice of____ praise,____ Christ our God,____ to thee we raise____ This our

57 sa - cri - fice of____ praise.

61 DESCANT SOPRANOS *f*
4. For each per - fect gift of thine To our race so____

ALL OTHER VOICES *f*
4. For each per - fect gift of thine To our race so free - ly

4. Gratitude

Henry van Dyke (1852–1933)

BOB CHILCOTT

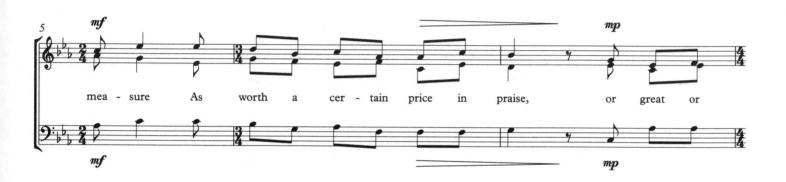

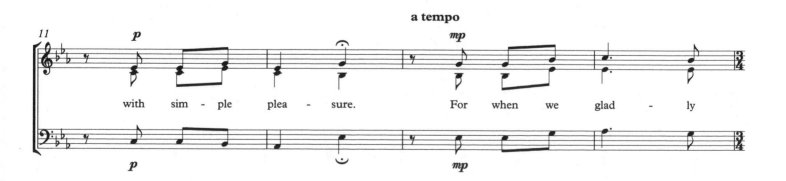

5. Hymn: Pray that Jerusalem may have peace

Scottish Psalter (1650)

BOB CHILCOTT

'PATE'

6. King of Glory, King of Peace

George Herbert (1593–1633)
from *The Temple* (1633)

BOB CHILCOTT

I will love___ thee:___ And that love_ may ne - ver cease,___ I will_ move___ thee.___

S. Where - fore_ with my_ ut - most art___ I will sing___ thee,___

A. Where - fore_ with my ut - most art___ I will sing___ thee,___

thee,_ And the_ cream of_ all_ my heart___ I will bring_ thee.___

And the_ cream of_ all my heart___ I will bring_ thee.___

7. Hymn: Through all the changing scenes of life

Nahum Tate (1652–1715) and Nicholas Brady (1659–1726)
New Version of the Psalms of David (1696)

BOB CHILCOTT

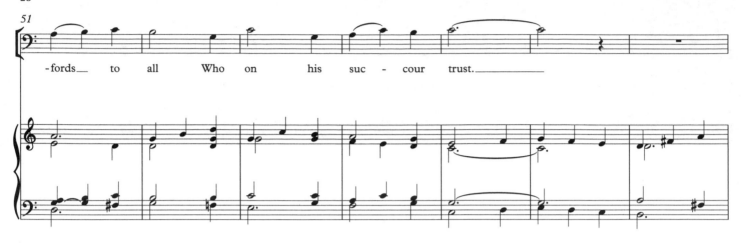

-fords__ to all Who on his suc - cour trust.__

S./A.

4. O make__ but tri - al of his love, Ex - pe - rience will de -

-cide_____ How blest__ they are,__ and on - ly they, Who in his

truth____ con - fide._____ 5. Fear him,____ ye

(ORG.) saints,___ and you___ will then___ Have no - thing else___ to fear;_____ Make

(ORG.) you____ his ser - vice your___ de - light,___ Your wants___ shall be___ his

in loving memory, Shauni McGregor

8. Consider

Christina Rossetti (1830–94)

BOB CHILCOTT

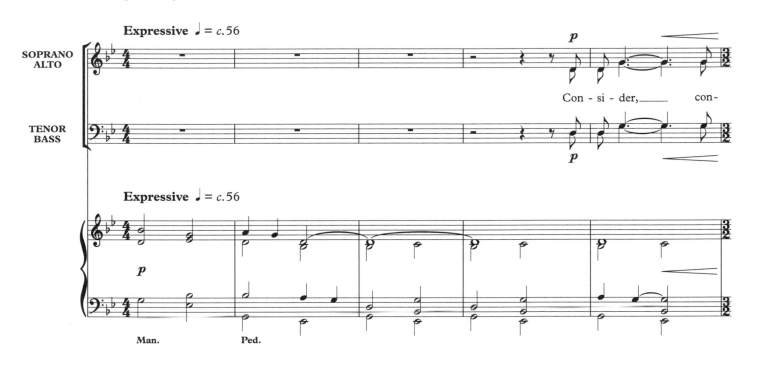

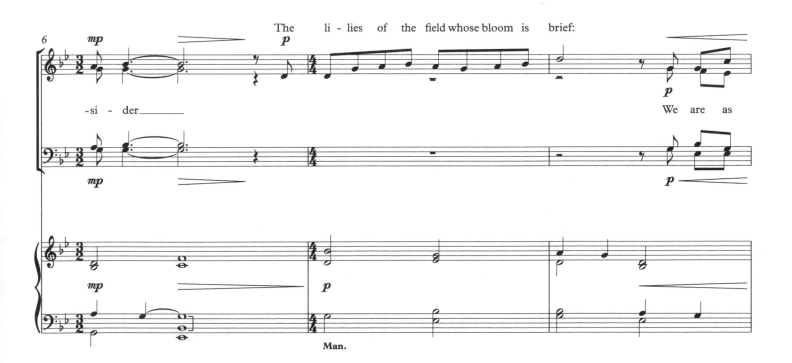

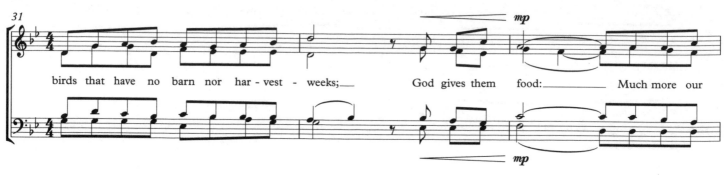

birds that have no barn nor har-vest - weeks;___ God gives them food:___ Much more our

Fa-ther seeks To do us good,___ Much more our Fa-ther seeks___ To do us good, to do us

good, us

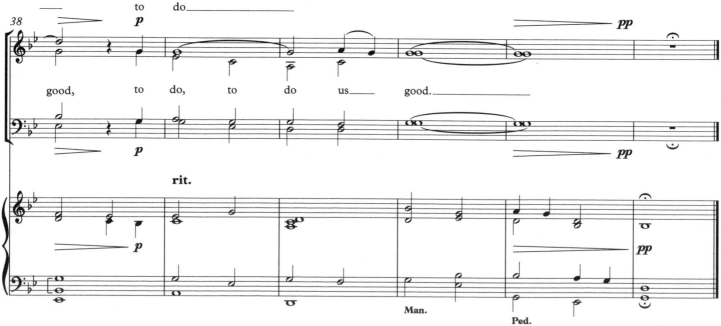

rit.

to do___

good, to do, to do us___ good.___

Man.   Ped.

9. Hymn: Now thank we all our God

Martin Rinkart (1586–1649)
trans. Catherine Winkworth (1827–78)

BOB CHILCOTT

'PICKER'

free___ us from___ all___ ills_____ In___ this___ world___ and_____ the

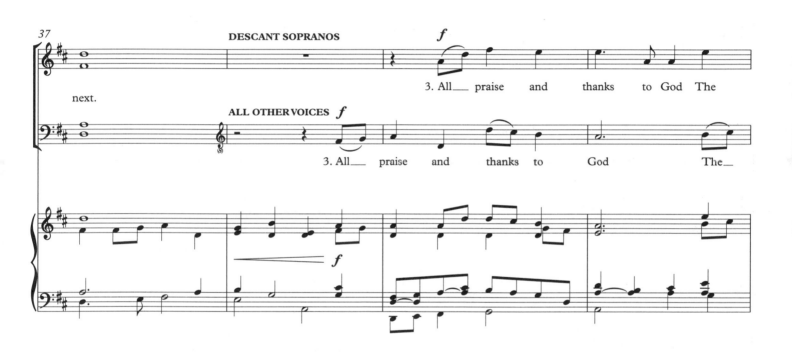

DESCANT SOPRANOS *f*

next. 3. All___ praise and thanks to God The

ALL OTHER VOICES *f*

3. All___ praise and thanks to God The___

Fa - ther___ now___ be gi - ven, The___ Son, and him who reigns With

Fa - ther now___ be___ gi - ven, The___ Son, and him___ who reigns With___